E. J. BEDFORD

of

LEWES

PHOTOGRAPHER OF THE
LONDON BRIGHTON & SOUTH COAST RAILWAY

JOHN MINNIS

WILD SWAN PUBLICATIONS LTD

For
JOHN E. KITE
who first awakened my interest
in the work of E. J. Bedford

ACKNOWLEDGEMENTS

I should like to thank firstly John E. Kite, who provided me with many original Bedford prints. M. J. Crutten-den kindly allowed me to copy his Bedford lantern slides and has supplied much additional background information. I am also indebted to him for reading through the manuscript. Mrs. Z. Rector of the Sussex Archaeological Society showed me the society's collection of Bedford prints and notebooks and, much to my delight, managed to find a picture of Bedford himself.

C. P. Atkins and T. J. Edgington of the National Railway Museum have given every assistance and I should also thank the Keeper of the Museum for permission to reproduce some of the views listed below. Ian Dawson lent me one photograph which has not turned up elsewhere and Kenneth H. Leech let me copy some fascinating correspondence he had with Bedford just after the Second World War. As always, I owe a great debt to the late D. L. Bradley's splendid trilogy on LB & SCR Locomotives from which much of the factual material was derived.

Finally, Paul Karau has made many helpful suggestions as to the style and layout of the book, and I should like to thank him and June Judge for their hospitality.

National Railway Museum, Crown Copyright
Plates 11, 16, 24, 27, 35, 50, 66, 84, 85, 88, 89, 98-102, 107, 114-116, 119-122, 124-126, 134, 137-139, 140-142.

E. J. Bedford prints
Plates 4, 7, 8-10, 12-15, 17-21, 23, 25, 26, 28-34, 36-49, 51-55, 57, 58, 60, 62-65, 67-69, 72-74, 76-78, 80, 81, 86, 87, 90-97, 103-106, 108, 113, 117, 118, 123, 127-133, 135, 136, 143-145

E. J. Bedford lantern slides, courtesy M. J. Cruttenden
Plates 22, 56, 59, 61, 70, 71, 75, 79, 82, 83, 109-112

Lens of Sutton
Plate 6

Sussex Archaeological Society
Plates 1, 2, 3

Designed by Paul Karau
Typesetting by Berkshire Publishing Services
Printed by Amadeus Press Ltd., Huddersfield

Published by
WILD SWAN PUBLICATIONS LTD.
1-3 Hagbourne Road, Didcot, Oxon OX11 8DP

E. J. BEDFORD

A BIOGRAPHICAL INTRODUCTION

EDWARD John Bedford was born in Lewes in the mid-1860s, the son of a tax-collector. By the early '70s, the family were living in a newly constructed four-storey terraced house at 11 St. John's Terrace, Lewes. The house was located in a pleasant middle-class area which was close to the centre of the town, yet, bounded as it was by the water meadows of the River Ouse, remained within a few minutes walk of open country. By looking out of the windows of the upper floors of the house, the view was closed by the South Downs and, closer to hand, ran the main line of the London Brighton and South Coast Railway from London to Newhaven and Eastbourne which emerged from a tunnel under the town. Both these elements, the proximity of the natural landscape and of the Brighton Railway were to be an influence on the young Bedford.

There is a tendency for a biography, when our knowledge of the subject's life is limited, to resemble a catalogue at times and I am afraid that of Bedford is no exception. But a knowledge of his career is essential if we are to understand his photographic ambitions and style. He became a pupil of the Lewes School of Art in Albion Street where he showed considerable promise. His talents led him to take up a career in teaching art and he became a master at Brighton School of Art in 1883.[1] It was during this period in the mid-1880s that he took up the hobby of photography, something that he saw as being both an art in itself and a tool that he could put to good use. Like most amateur photographers, he took conventional studies of landscapes and picturesque old cottages. But it was his use of photography to serve his other interests that distinguishes him from many of his contemporaries. A keen antiquarian (he had joined the Sussex Archaeological Society in 1890 and was its longest serving member at the time of his death), he made a photographic record of events in his home town and of change within it. These pictures included views of the 1892 Parliamentary Election, the Lewes floods of the preceding year and numerous examples of historic buildings in the town, especially those about to disappear. Some of his finest photographs in this genre were those of the 1891 Sheep Fair, capturing the

Plate 1. E. J. Bedford.

be-smocked Sussex shepherds to good effect.[2] The Lewes Photographic Society was established in 1888 and Bedford served as its Honorary Secretary until 1891, giving regular lectures to its members.

Natural history was Bedford's principal interest and it was in this field that he made his name as a photographer. Elected a Fellow of the Royal Photographic Society, he exhibited work regularly, gave lectures and wrote articles on his two specialisms, birds and orchids. In 1909, J. M. Dent published *Nature Photography for Beginners*, a lavish work with 100 illustrations from his photographs.

Returning to Bedford's teaching career, early in 1892 he was appointed Headmaster of the Eastbourne Municipal School of Art and Design.[3] To be nearer his work, he moved around 1901 to 'Anderida', 13 Gorringe Road, Eastbourne, a substantial house in the fashionable Upperton district where he was to remain until about 1917.[4] After many years at the school, he decided to set up on his own account, a handbill dated 21st January 1915 announcing that he would be holding classes in the studio of the late artist, J. Haynes Williams. This arrangement did not last long for by the early twenties, he was back at the Lewes School of Art as its Principal.

During this period he was energetically photographing natural history subjects and contributed a series of articles on orchids to the early numbers of the *Sussex County Magazine*.[5] He became more fully involved in the life of his town. A Scientific and Literary Society was formed largely at his instigation and, under his secretaryship, flourished throughout the inter-war years. In the twenties and thirties, he resumed the work of recording old buildings that had been forsaken in favour of nature photography between 1900 and 1920. Many of these pictures were reproduced in *The Official Guide to Lewes*, edited by his friend, Walter H. Godfrey. This guide, reprinted many times since its publication in the 1930s and commended as 'a paragon of its kind' by Sir Nikolaus Pevsner, was prepared under the auspices of a committee whose membership included Bedford, who was responsible for a chapter on the natural history of the district in which he expressed his love for the Sussex downland. Much of his time, however, was taken up by his duties as

Plate 2. The best known of all Bedford's photographs — his picture of a discussion about Southdown sheep at the Lewes Sheep Fair of 1891, which has become something of a classic of rural life.

part-time curator of the Lewes Borough Museum set up in the old Market Tower in July 1921. He worked for two days a week at a salary of 10/-. The job was no sinecure, the Minutes of the Museum Sub-Committee of the Borough Council frequently containing references to the lack of space and dampness of the premises. The closure of the art school in 1932 enabled the Museum to be established on a more permanent basis, taking over the former premises in Albion Street and with Bedford appointed as full-time curator at £120 per annum.[6] The new museum was opened on 26th November 1934 and Bedford stayed in the post until his retirement at the end of 1950. The museum, under Bedford's direction, was a traditional local museum with a mixture of exhibits, the emphasis being on archaeology and natural history. The Minutes solemnly record the gift of such treasures as a stuffed duck-billed platypus. A hostile councillor's suggestion in 1947 that 'the exhibits were dusty, musty and fusty' was quickly refuted by the Museum Sub-Committee. The museum that had been so important in Bedford's life closed in the 1950s, the building subsequently being used as Lewes Library.

Despite advancing years, Bedford remained active in photographic and natural history circles, lecturing as late as 1946 on wild flowers to the Royal Photographic Society in London. When death came, it was in rather macabre circumstances. On Friday, 6th February 1953, police forced an entry to his house in St. John's Terrace where they found him lying dead on an upstairs landing and the body of his housekeeper, Miss Flora Barden, in the basement kitchen. Both had been dead since Wednesday. The Coroner was unable to say who had died first and recorded a verdict of misadventure on Bedford and natural causes on Miss Barden. The report of the incident filled much of the front page of the *Sussex Express* and his obituary (which was a detailed affair in those days of reflective local newspapers) recorded that he was ' . . . an expert in natural history (especially insect and bird life), a brilliant photographer (particularly in the field of nature), and was clever with pen and brush.'[7]

Of his personality, we know little. He was apparently very jealous of his photographs; John Kite recounts the story that he always had to be present when a print was made from his negatives so as to ensure that no unauthorised copies were run off! His interests were wide-ranging; besides art, natural history and railways, he played the organ at both Cliffe and Glynde churches and at Lewes prison.

RAILWAY PHOTOGRAPHY
To understand the importance of Bedford's work, we need to look briefly at the development of railway photography up to the period 1888-1892 when he first became active in the field and, in particular, study the progress made in capturing trains travelling at speed.

The overwhelming majority of railway photographs taken prior to the 1890s were the responsibility of the railway companies themselves, either taken directly by their own photographers or by outside contractors at their behest. Stations and viaducts were sometimes included in the catalogues of professional photographers of views and landscapes. Due to the cost of the equipment and the difficulties inherent in the wet-collodion process, amateur photographers in general were relatively few in number and were attracted to portraits and pastoral scenes rather than such prosaic mechanical subjects as trains.

It was only when dry plates began to be widely available that amateur photography became a popular hobby and it became possible to take successful photographs of moving objects in the 1880s with the introduction of faster shutters, such photographs being known at the time as 'instantaneous' pictures. The first amateur railway photographer whose name has come down to us is R. H. Bleasdale of Warwick, whose work which began late in the '60s, consisted of views of solo locomotives. He covered much of the country in a series of annual tours, taking some 3,000 photographs and his negatives still exist in some profusion; the Manchester Model Railway Society, the National Railway Museum and the Locomotive Publishing Company (now owned by Ian Allan Ltd) all have examples of his work.[8] When was the first successful photograph of a train moving at speed taken? There is no clear answer as so few photographs can be positively dated. The earliest to come to light is a rather blurred view of the Great Western Railway's royal train passing Olton, near Birmingham, on 23rd March 1887.[9] Another claimant to the title is Cameron Swan's picture of LC & DR *Frolic* at Bromley, which is considered to have been taken in October 1885. His two views of expresses at Sandy station on the Great Northern Railway main line, which were reproduced in C. H. Grinling's *History of the Great Northern Railway*, are precisely dated (1st August 1887)[11] They are of excellent quality, well composed with little blurring due to the speed of the engine. The problem of stopping the motion was a very real one when both camera and emulsion speeds were limited. P. W. Pilcher, a master at Shrewsbury School, took a photograph of a Sturrock 2—2—2 near Boston in 1889 which he felt was one of the earliest examples of 'panning' or swinging the camera to keep the locomotive sharp.[12] Pilcher was a great innovator, choosing unusual angles, such as from the top or the rear, to make attractive studies. In doing this, he was the forerunner of the modern school of photography represented by such fine practitioners as G. F. Heiron or C. T. Gifford; it is a great misfortune that, having his photographs issued by the Locomotive Publishing Co., they are seldom acknowledged to him. Besides Bedford, the other pioneers of action railway photography include Dr. Tice F. Budden, who took up photography as an undergraduate at Cambridge in 1889 and Rev. A. H. Malan. Budden's early work included a selection of photographs taken at Ealing in the last years of the broad gauge and, like Bedford, he was active for many years, his last pictures being near his home at Dorking just after the Second World War. Malan, too, found his inspiration in the impending demise of the Great Western broad gauge. Although he photographed stationary locomotives as early as 1883, he did not turn to action photography until 1891/2.[13]

E. J. BEDFORD, THE PHOTOGRAPHER

The earliest positively dated railway photograph by Bedford was taken in 1888 (*Plate 12*) although it is probable that his views of the 1857 Lewes station were taken a couple of years earlier. He started to take pictures of moving trains the following year at Haywards Heath (*Plates 85-86*) and it would seem that these views were taken largely as an experiment. Interested in the technical aspects of photography, he was anxious to see what could be achieved using the latest advances. His captions to the lantern slides he prepared (travelling at 60 mph) bear this out; it also suggests why the range of locations was limited. To try and stop the motion using a relatively slow shutter speed, he took the photograph at a fairly acute angle with the train only forming a small part of the negative (*Plate 67*); if he deviated from these rules, the results tended to be blurred (*Plates 65, 88*). He had a gift for posing a locomotive with an uncluttered background and usually found an angle where the wheels and detail under the footplate, which tended to disappear into deep shadow, were illuminated by the sun (*Plates 7, 32*).

The geographical area covered was small, the majority of the photographs being taken at Lewes, Cooksbridge and Newhaven, with occasional visits to Brighton, Hastings, Shoreham and Haywards Heath. In a period when equipment was bulky and travel expensive, this is perhaps not surprising. However, he did manage a limited number of views on other railways, all taken in outer London suburbs, probably while he was in London for the day. As I have suggested, some of the moving train photographs were experiments. But this is not to say that Bedford had no interest in the subject matter. He was both knowledgeable and interested in railways, particularly locomotives. This interest was not nostalgic; he wrote many years later to Kenneth H. Leech:

> 'I am afraid I was like some others you mention; and always wanted to photograph the latest types. I regret now, that I did not secure some of the older types, especially of the LB & SC Railway. There are very few of these about and they would be most interesting now.'[14]

This poses an interesting question. Why should a man whose great interest in life was natural history and who, with his liking of old churches, cottages, and so on, was an antiquarian at heart, be interested in railways, particularly in the latest locomotives and the high speed expresses, something that one might reasonably think would be anathema to him? After all, the conservationist of today rarely has an enthusiasm for juggernauts! The clue to his interest is, I believe, to be found in his artistic nature. I would argue that the LB & SCR's celebrated Locomotive Superintendent, William Stroudley's flair as a designer and the brilliance of the extraordinary ochre shade employed by him attracted Bedford as a fellow artist. It is no coincidence that Stroudley was on the Board of Governors of the Brighton School of Art where Bedford taught. A further factor that lends support to this argument is that Bedford was not the only artist to be attracted by the beautiful appearance of the LB & SCR's locomotives. Eric Gill, who spent much of his childhood in Brighton, made large numbers of paintings and drawings of LB & SCR locomotives: ' . . . it was the shape and character of the locomotive that really enthralled me.'[15] The LB & SCR practice of painting the engine names in superbly executed lettering (for many years the work of George Thompson) may have awakened an interest in lettering that was to lead in time to the Gill Sans alphabet. Bedford was therefore in good company in his liking for the rather exotic looking Stroudley engines.

In his lifetime, Bedford's railway photographs were rarely reproduced, his moving train photographs being occasionally employed to illustrate articles in the *Railway Magazine* in the early 1900s. In 1935, he supplied several series of photographs for the part-work *Railway Wonders of the World*. A number of his Lewes photographs accompanied Charles E. Lee's article 'The Lewes Station Mystery' in the *Railway Magazine* (Volume 94, January 1950) but it was not until John E. Kite reproduced two of his finest pictures in that splendid tribute to the early photographers *1850-1925 Vintage Album* that the quality of his work was recognised. As a result, his photographs have not received the attention they deserve and the bulk of them are published here for the first time.

The history of his photographs following his death reads at times a little like a detective story. On his death, his personal collection of prints was acquired by John Kite and is now in my possession. The negatives, together with those of G. F. Burtt and the Chambers brothers passed to a Mr. Hammond of Hove and remained inaccessible for many years.

Bedford for his lectures, and, consequently, the quality does vary a little. I have indicated against those prints where a negative is held by the National Railway Museum, the appropriate NRM Burtt collection negative numbers, so that the book may also serve as, in effect, a catalogue to the Museum's holding.

Plate 3. The elephants of Lord George Ginnett's Circus make their way along Friars Walk on 24th July 1891. This is a typical example of Bedford recording notable local events with his camera. In the background is the old Friars Walk terminus and, behind the elephants, the Fitzroy Library.

They were widely assumed to have been lost. In the meantime, Michael Cruttenden and I were visiting the well-known antiquarian bookseller, Norman Kerr of Cartmel, and were about to leave when a large quantity of lantern slides was discovered in a box on the floor. These proved to be the work of Bedford and were speedily acquired. In 1982, the Burtt collection, which included the Bedford negatives, came up for auction and was acquired by the National Railway Museum. It is fortunate that after so many vicissitudes, the negatives are now preserved. Not all of Bedford's negatives reached York; there are numerous photographs that exist only as original Bedford prints or lantern slides. The York negatives are not separately listed; however, identification by style of print and negative number is not difficult.

The present work is intended as a *catalogue raisonné* of Bedford's railway photography; all his known photographs have been included with the exception of a limited number of views that I have been unable to trace. These include some pictures taken during the 1930s of LMS and LNER streamliners, George V's funeral train, and GNR No. 1 in 1938, which were the last railway subjects that Bedford took. His notebooks contain a number of brief, tantalising references to other railway negatives and it is quite possible that other Bedford photographs may come to light. I should be most interested to hear of them. Because I have made an attempt to represent Bedford's complete output, the collection may seem to lack balance, but it reflects what happened to interest a pioneer railway photographer. The originals from which the reproductions in this book have been made, have come from a variety of sources, prints made by E. J. Bedford himself, National Railway Museum prints, and lantern slides produced by

NOTES

1. *Sussex Express & County Herald*, 13th February 1953.
2. Bedford's negatives of Sussex subjects and some relating to natural history are held by the Sussex Archaeological Society, Barbican House, Lewes. The Society also has in its possession eight of his photographic notebooks, in which he meticulously recorded the date and exposure details of each of his photographs. Unfortunately, all but one of the notebooks covering the period 1888-1892, when he took the majority of his railway photographs, are missing.
3. *Sussex Express & County Herald*, 16th January 1892.
4. Information derived from *Pike's Eastbourne Directory*.
5. 'Sussex Orchids', *Sussex County Magazine* Vol. 1, 5-10 (April-September 1927).
6. Lewes Borough Council, Minute Book of Museum Sub-Committee, 7th May 1934, East Sussex Record Office BLE/A3/586.
7. *Sussex Express & County Herald*, 13th February 1953.
8. There is a useful note on Bleasdale in *The Locomotive* Vol. 30, 15th August 1924, pp. 249-50.
9. P. Kingston, *Royal Trains* (David & Charles 1985) p. 23.
10. J. E. Kite, *1850-1925 Vintage Album* (Roundhouse 1966).
11. C. H. Grinling, *History of the Great Northern Railway* (Methuen 1898) pp. 380-81.
12. Reproduced in Kite, *Vintage Album*.
13. An excellent selection of Dr. Budden's photographs which display the range of his work is in R. Bucknell and T. F. Budden, *Railway Memories* (Bucks Head Press 1947). Most, but not all, of his negatives are in the hands of Locomotive & General Railway Photographs. Malan's photographs are published in *Broad Gauge Finale* (Wild Swan 1985).
14. Letter of E. J. Bedford to K. H. Leech, 21st February 1946.
15. E. Gill, *Autobiography* (The Book Club edn. 1949) p. 74. Gill's drawings of LB & SCR engines are in the West Sussex Record Office.

Plate 4. A member of the remarkable and long-lived class 'A1', popularly known as 'Terriers' or 'Rooters', No. 41 *Piccadilly* waits between turns at Kemp Town station. It was built in June 1877 and is seen here c.1895. Following a long period of storage at East Grinstead, the engine was broken up in 1902, one of the earlier members of the class to be withdrawn. One unusual feature is the background to the numberplate which appears to have been polished instead of following the standard practice of being painted blue. Wagons of the local coal merchant, C. M. Perkins, stand behind the locomotive, while the fireman on the left is Jack Fellingham, and next to him the driver, Charles Pont. *NRM Burtt 2540*

Plate 5. For some reason, Bedford repeated the photograph with the crew in a different position. *NRM Burtt 2541*

Plate 6. A third picture was taken, this time from a slightly different angle. This view is reproduced from a copy print and is consequently not up to the usual quality. There is a fourth version that is very similar; no print has been found. These were the only photographs that Bedford took at Kemp Town.

Plate 7. Forming one of the most beautiful photographs of a locomotive ever taken, No. 81 *Beulah* stands on the turntable at Lewes in the winter of 1893. The low sun has picked out the wheels and frames as surely as a spotlight. It is the use of a low camera position that makes the picture so successful; it serves to emphasise the perfect proportions of Stroudley's design and gives the little engine greater dignity than its dimensions would suggest. *Beulah* was one of the final batch of 'Terriers' built in 1880, distinguished by their cast-iron brake blocks from earlier examples which employed wood. It was named after Beulah Hill, a district near Norwood in south London which was in later years the home of O. J. Morris, a great 'Brighton' devotee.

NRM Burtt 2536

Plate 8. Another view of No. 81 standing in the platforms of Lewes station. The date is a little earlier than the previous photo as it was taken before the station was rebuilt. As in many of Bedford's portraits, the crew posed with their engine and have been joined by an inspector and a porter. The inspector is William Hayder who was Lewes platform inspector from 1876 until his retirement in October 1897. Lansdown Place is in the background with Miss Mary Smith's agency for servants on the left and the premises of a tanners in the centre.

NRM Burtt 2537

Plate 9. Most photographers of railways in the nineteenth century were conventional in their approach and so was Bedford as a rule. This view is something out of the ordinary in that Bedford broke with the usual practice of photographing locomotives from the front. Built the same year as *Beulah* and of identical appearance, No. 84 *Crowborough* is posed at an unknown location in 1892.

NRM Burtt 2538

Plate 10. Besides taking photographs himself, Bedford occasionally copied the work of others, in this case a well-known official photograph of No. 40 *Brighton*, probably taken on the engine's return from its triumph at the Paris Exhibition of 1878. Other versions of the photograph exist, the best being one with a very dapper William Stroudley standing in front of his creation. *NRM Burtt 3387*

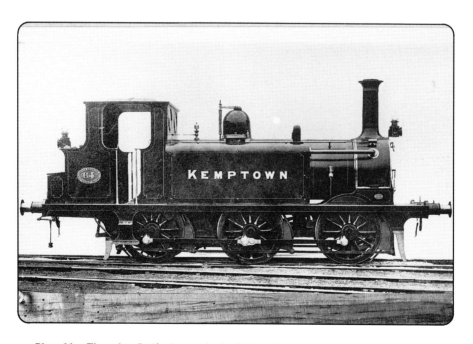

Plate 11. The other Bedford copy in the National Railway Museum collection is this photograph of No. 64 *Kemptown*. The original photograph probably dates from 1874 when the engine was built; just why Bedford decided to copy these two views is unknown. Two features in the photograph are of interest: the use of one word rather than two for Kemp Town (a practice favoured by the LB & SCR's signwriter) and the lamp with the engine number painted on it, a convention that ceased in the early 1900s. *NRM Burtt 3388*

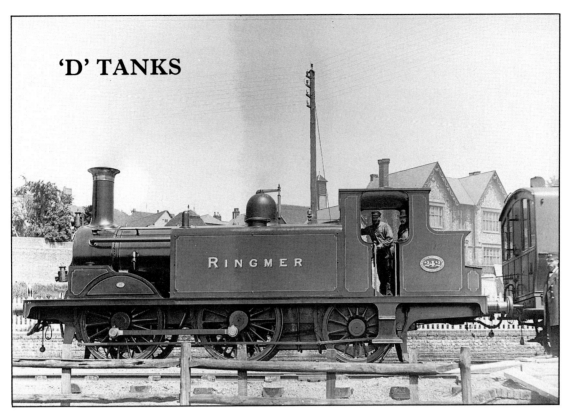

'D' TANKS

Plate 12. The most numerous of all the LB & SCR engines were the 'D' tanks. 'D1' No. 242 *Ringmer*, one of the batch built by Neilson & Co. in 1881, posed with crew and guard for this, one of the first of Bedford's locomotive portraits at the up London platform of Lewes station in 1888. *Ringmer* was scrapped in July 1925. Behind the engine are the Central National Schools of 1843, an attractive building that still exists but threatened at the time of writing with demolition.

Plate 13. Although the environs of Tunbridge Wells engine shed were to prove popular with photographers of locomotives in the early years of the present century, Bedford only appears to have paid one visit there when he secured this portrait of 'D' tank No. 232 *Lewes*. One of the penultimate batch of what was the largest class of engine south of the Thames, it was built in 1884. This view was copied and issued by O. J. Morris as a postcard between the wars. *NRM Burtt 3439*

Plate 14. *Lewes* again, appropriately enough at Lewes. The turntable was a favourite prop of Bedford's. These Stroudley engines looked elegant from almost any angle.

NRM Burtt 3440

Plate 15. No. 235 *Broadwater* at the west end of Lewes station in 1892. One of 35 built by Neilson & Co. in Glasgow, it arrived at Brighton in 1881. This was another view copied by O.J. Morris.

NRM Burtt 3440

Plate 16. One of the earlier 'D' tanks, No. 296 *Osborne* at Fratton engine shed. It still retains the wooden brake blocks that were superseded by cast iron in 1880 and, although the paint around the feed pump has been burnt away, note how the bare metal has been polished. It took 2¾ hours for a cleaner and his mate to clean a 'D' tank and Stroudley was criticized for the amount spent on engine cleaning. His reply was that clean engines were a good advertisement for the company. *Osborne* received the more prosaic name *Peckham* in 1901 when a new Billinton 'B4' class express locomotive appeared bearing the name of the royal residence. Behind the engine is a line of locomotive coal wagons belonging to Messrs. Stephenson Clarke, contractors to the LB & SCR for this purpose, and beyond them one can just make out the cab of a LSWR locomotive.

NRM Burtt 2534

SINGLES

Plate 17. The unique No. 326 *Grosvenor*, Stroudley's large single of 1874, receives lubrication while standing in the old station at Lewes in 1888. The bright object below the footplate near the firebox is a speed indicator, a device that Stroudley invented, but its use was not widely extended. An example of Stroudley's patent speed indicator may be seen in the Science Museum, South Kensington. Behind the chimney is the New Station Inn (demolished in 1963 to provide better visibility at the busy junction with Station Road) and the Central National School of 1843. *NRM Burtt 1037*

Plate 18. A much later view of *Grosvenor* at Eastbourne. The date is post-1900 as the station nameboard is of the later pattern with cut-out rather than painted letters. The engine was withdrawn in 1907. *NRM Burtt 3390*

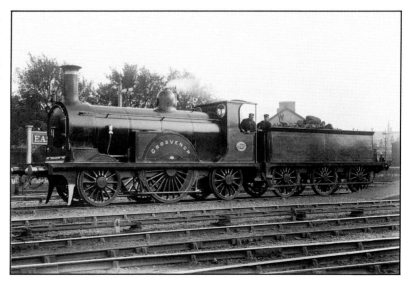

Plate 19. In 1876 a second single, No. 325 *Abergavenny*, was constructed as, in effect, a smaller version of *Grosvenor*. For some years it worked the up morning Continental from Newhaven where it is seen here bearing the appropriate double diamond headcode. Like *Grosvenor*, it is fitted with a speed indicator. In the background is one of the freight transhipment sheds and a four plank 'Open D' wagon.

NRM Burtt 2535

Plate 20. What may be termed the 'production version' of the Stroudley single was the 'G' class of 1880-82. No. 328 *Sutherland* takes water at Lewes towards the end of the 1890s. The engine has had its original wrought-iron driving wheels replaced with cast steel ones, recognisable by the crescent-shaped balance weights. This change took place gradually from 1894. The paintwork is looking a little shabby and that on the chimney and smokebox is burnt. *NRM Burtt 1038*

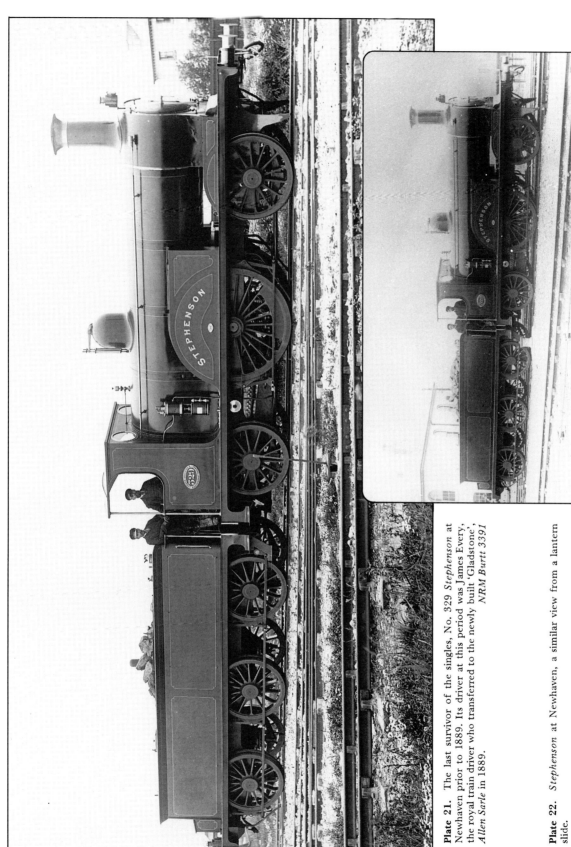

Plate 21. The last survivor of the singles, No. 329 *Stephenson* at Newhaven prior to 1889. Its driver at this period was James Every, the royal train driver who transferred to the newly built 'Gladstone', *Allen Sarle* in 1889.
NRM Burtt 3391

Plate 22. *Stephenson* at Newhaven, a similar view from a lantern slide.

'LYONS' CLASS

Plate 23. A member of the 1883 batch of the small 'Lyons' class of mixed traffic 0—4—2s, No. 313 *Paris*, stands at Newhaven. Based at New Cross shed, it was used on the Grande and Petite Vitesse services. These services (the Grande ran daily from Dieppe and the Petite three times weekly from Caen) were mainly for perishable traffic. Seasonal fruit traffic made up the greater part of the loads, either from France or from merchant ships docking at Newhaven. The service was sub-contracted to the engine's driver, Holbrook, who was provided with the engine, coal, water and other stores and was paid an agreed sum each month, out of which he had to pay the fireman and cleaner. The building behind the engine is described on the original contract drawing as 'rooms for workmen' and was put up in 1886, while a passengers' luggage van No. 221 is just visible on the left. Beneath the cab footplate is a capstan used for shunting wagons.   *NRM Burtt 3386*

'GLADSTONES'

Plate 24. The pinnacle of Stroudley's work were the 'Gladstones'. No. 179 *Sandown* poses with its crew at Newhaven, probably soon after the engine entered service in 1890. *NRM Burtt 3434*

Plate 25. The brand new *Allen Sarle* stands at Newhaven (note the ships' masts to the rear) with its driver James Every in 1889. The engine was named after the LB & SCR's Secretary (appointed 1867) who became General Manager in 1886. Sir Allen Sarle retired from both posts in 1897 and was made a director. Newhaven appealed to Bedford as he was able to obtain an uncluttered background for his portraits. *NRM Burtt 2542*

Plate 26. No. 189 *Edward Blount* on Lewes turntable c.1892. The engine had been exhibited at the Paris Exhibition of 1889 where it was awarded a gold medal, a fact recorded on the trailing splashers. Sir Edward Blount was a notable financier responsible for much railway construction on the continent from the 1840s in partnership with men such as Samuel Laing and Thomas Brassey. He lived in LB & SCR territory at Imberhorne Manor, near East Grinstead, and was Chairman of the Western Railway of France with which the Brighton Railway enjoyed a close working relationship. He was also a director of the Paris, Lyons and Mediterranean Railway on whose lines the engine was tested in January 1890 after the closure of the Paris Exhibition. The brickwork in the background is the drive to 'Leighside' which crossed the old main line at this point.

NRM Burtt 2544

Plate 27. A second view of *Edward Blount* near the goods yard at Lewes, the building in the background being the tranship shed. The London & South Western Railway wagon on the left is of the 1872 Beattie design and is in the pre-1890 lettering style. On the right, a rather well-worn LB & SCR open displays what is often referred to as the 'illiterate' symbol used prior to the introduction of the company's initials on wagon sides c.1895. In fact, the term is something of a misnomer as all LB & SCR employees were required to be able to read and write, a condition of employment laid down as early as 1839.

NRM Burtt 2543

Plate 28. No. 195 *Cardew* seen at Newhaven soon after construction in 1888. At this time, the engine was used on the evening Newhaven boat train and run under contract by its driver.

NRM Burtt 3433

Plate 29. Strictly outside LB & SCR territory, No. 198 *Sheffield* (named after Lord Sheffield of Sheffield Park) at Hastings c.1890. Newly built Braybrooke Terrace is visible behind. A mechanically operated scotch block, intended to prevent wagon runaways, is in the foreground.

NRM Burtt 3431

Plate 30. No. 218 *Beaconsfield*, with its smokebox door decorated for a Primrose League excursion, outside St. Leonards shed. The engine was named after the Conservative prime minister, the Earl of Beaconsfield (Benjamin Disraeli) who was elevated to the peerage in 1876. The large houses, in the tiled and half-timbered style so characteristic of the period, comprise the Convalescent Home for Poor Children opened in 1882.   *NRM Burtt 3430*

Plate 31. *Beaconsfield* again, at the head of the Primrose League special in Hastings station. The Primrose League was founded in 1883 by Sir George Birdwood taking the Earl of Beaconsfield's favourite flower as its emblem. One of the League's main objectives was to involve more women in political activities. Special trains to raise funds were run on Primrose Day each year to commemorate the Earl's death on 19th April 1881.
NRM Burtt 3429

Plate 32. An immaculate No. 220 *Hampden* at Hastings, a little earlier than the photograph of *Sheffield*; the house in Linton Road has only reached the ground floor level. The engine's namesake, Viscount Hampden of Glynde Place, who was created a peer in 1884, was Lord Lieutenant of Sussex and a director of the Newhaven Harbour Company.

NRM Burtt 3432

STATION MASTERS' AND INSPECTORS' EXCURSIONS

Among the many excursion trains that were put on by the LB & SCR, the most notable, certainly in visual terms, were those run in aid of the Station Masters' and Inspectors' Mutual Aid and Widows Fund, which was established as a superannuation fund in 1874 and, with only one exception, ran its fund-raising excursions from London to Eastbourne from 1877 to 1914. The fund was administered by an elected chairman, secretary and committee, the chairman being the senior station master on the system which, for the great part of the fund's existence, was Robert Pierpoint, Station Superin-

tendent at London Bridge, who held the position until his retirement.

In 1898, seven special trains, carrying nearly 3,000 people at 4/- each were provided, two from Victoria and one each from London Bridge, New Cross, Sutton, Croydon and Horsham. The excursion, normally held in mid-June, was brought forward to 16th May because of the Whitsun holiday and the crowd enjoyed good weather. The revellers were accompanied by the band of M Division of the Metropolitan Police, who formed up outside Eastbourne station where they played a

Plate 33. *Allen Sarle*, the Battersea-based engine of the Victoria train, poses on the turntable of the Eastbourne roundhouse with driver John Avery and his fireman, Henry Osborne. There can have been few more extraordinary, not to say dazzling, sights in late Victorian England than the engine so embellished in full flight. Both engine and tender are bedecked with various representations of the LB & SCR's heraldic devices — crests on the engine, shields on the tender. The plaster figures flank the headboard and even the coal is whitewashed — a practice usually reserved for royal trains. *NRM Burtt 2547*

programme of music before moving with the assembled throng to the pier, where they played at the Pavilion for a further hour. While the excursionists played cricket or skated in Devonshire Park, admission to which was included in the price of their tickets, or simply sat on the beach, the Committee of the Fund and their guests had 'a sumptuous lunch' at the Gildredge Hotel, presided over by the Fund's Chairman, Robert Pierpoint. The festivities continued until the first train left for home soon after 7 p.m.

The attitude of the people of Eastbourne to this influx was expressed by 'Boreas' in his column 'Pith and Point' in the *Eastbourne Gazette*. He described the excursion as 'a great success' and echoed feelings of relief about good behaviour:

'. . . everybody and everything was highly decorous and de rigger [*sic*] so to speak . . . . There was no rowdyism, no drunkenness, and certainly no jinks of a can-canny nature.'

While the wealthy shopkeepers of Terminus Road might be disparaging of the day tripper, 'Boreas' was sure that they had done very well out of him.

The tradition grew up that the engine hauling the London Bridge train and that of the first train from Victoria should be decorated. There was keen rivalry between New Cross and Battersea engine sheds over who could provide the most spectacular decoration. In 1898, a Sunday newspaper offered a prize and this inspired J. J. Richardson, the Battersea District Locomotive Superintendent to purchase two gilded plaster figures from a travelling showman who had pitched his tents near Richardson's official residence in Queens Road, Battersea, so as to ensure victory. In this he succeeded although 'Boreas' was even-handed in his praise, 'any one of the decorated engines would have taken first place at the Battle of Flowers.'

Plate 34. The rival New Cross locomotive No. 203 *Henry Fletcher*, designed by Stroudley's successor, R. J. Billinton, was one of the pretty but, by all accounts, ineffectual 'B2s'. *Henry Fletcher* was named after Sir Henry Aubrey Fletcher, Bart., Fourth Baronet of Ham Manor, Angmering (1835-1910), MP for Lewes 1880-1910. Rampant dragons replace the plaster figures while the double diamond headcode disc, indicating that the train is a special, is incorporated in the design of the decoration. The slope of the footplate is covered in what may almost be described as carpet bedding. Driver Sargent stands on the footplate, below him on the left is Edwin Trangmar, the New Cross District Locomotive Superintendent responsible for the decorations. Trangmar, the former Chief Clerk at Brighton locomotive works, had been appointed to the New Cross post in February 1874 which he held until his retirement in 1899. He was also chairman of the railway's Provident Society; he died in October 1911.
NRM Burtt 2548

Plate 35. The two locomotives together. *NRM Burtt 2549*

Plate 36. The contrasting engines make a fine display as they stand in the old Eastbourne roundhouse.

DIGNITY AND IMPUDENCE

Plate 37. 'Dignity and Impudence' photographs were always popular; the practice was to put together the smallest and largest locomotives of a railway so as to provide a contrast. *Beulah* and *Sandown*, both photographed individually by Bedford, represent Stroudley's most successful designs. The two are outside the new engine shed at Newhaven in 1892.

NRM Burtt 3435

SOME BILLINTON DESIGNS

Plate 38. The 'B2s' were proving to be poor performers and Billinton fitted the last of the type, No. 213 *Bessemer*, with a larger boiler. Its performance was not greatly improved and 213 was to remain the solitary example of what Marsh designated Class 'B3'. The engine is seen here at Eastbourne, probably soon after construction in 1897. It was rebuilt to Class 'B2X' in November 1908 and was withdrawn in 1930. *NRM Burtt 1110*

Plate 39. Bedford photographed the latest designs as they came out and he was interested in the new Billinton locomotives which represented such a change from Stroudley's work. No. 363 *Goldsmid*, the first of the 'D3' class, was pictured brand new in 1892. Sir Julian Goldsmid had been elected to the LB & SCR board on 30th September 1891. Following the death of Jonas Levy, the Deputy Chairman on 7th July 1894, Sir Julian acted in his place, but was himself taken seriously ill the following year and died on 7th January 1896. The engine only bore the name until 1895 when it was transferred to a new express locomotive, but its likeness, complete with original name, was a feature of LB & SCR enginemen's cap badges for many years. *NRM Burtt 2545*

Plate 40. *Victoria*, built a month later, stands at Bedford's favourite location of Lewes turntable, probably in the same year.

Plate 41. R. J. Billinton's goods engine, the 'C2', appeared in 1893. One of the last to be constructed, No. 550 poses when new in 1902 in the East Yard sidings at Lewes. The engine was rebuilt by Marsh with a larger boiler in November 1910 and lasted in this form as a 'C2X' until December 1961.

LEWES STATION

Bedford took a number of photographs of the 1857 station at Lewes shortly before it was rebuilt in 1889 and of the line to the east of it which was replaced for passenger traffic by a new route slightly further south (see map). Here we see Bedford, the local photographer, at work, for these pictures were, like so many of his photographs, taken as a local history record rather than purely for their railway interest. He also made a record of the 1846 station building which was by this time used by the goods department.

Plate 42. The imposing 1846 terminus building at Friars Walk, Lewes. Built by John Fabian of Brighton, it was a building very much in the style of its day, a rather heavy Italianate, and constructed of white bricks which were then the height of architectural fashion. The design should be compared with that at Chichester which was put up in the following year. If one was being critical, it may be suggested that the building looks a little like a rejected design for a corn market in a provincial town; the relationship between the three semi-circular first floor windows and the giant pilasters that bound them is unhappy and somewhat naive. Nonetheless, the station was an adornment to Lewes and its demolition in the 1960s is to be regretted. After standing empty for many years, a new magistrates court building has recently been built on the site.

Plate 43. The second station, built by J. Davey whose tender of £1,169 for the work was accepted by the LB & SCR Board on 30th April 1857. Although described as Gothic, the building was a creditable attempt at a Swiss chalet with deeply overhanging eaves. Surface treatment was most ornate with wooden beams flush set in the brickwork in a diapered pattern. On the right, beside the footbridge, is the engine shed.
NRM Burtt 1717

Plate 44. One of Bedford's best known photographs, having been frequently reproduced. It is stated to have been taken in 1888 but, as the reconstruction of the station commenced in February 1887, this and the next photograph must have been taken in the summer of 1886 at the latest. The station is a hive of activity with only the up London platform free. All the trains are composed of stock designed by Stroudley, with the exception of the leading luggage van in the Seaford branch train. The train from Brighton is drawn by a 'D' tank, that to Seaford by a 'Terrier', and the Eastbourne train has a 'Gladstone' at its head. The unusual construction of the station buildings can be seen, with wood panelling replacing the brick of the road elevation. To the left are Messrs. Chatfield's refreshment rooms, added a year after the main station buildings. The covered passage that gave access between the two sides of the station runs between these buildings and the refreshment rooms. Filling the space where the two lines diverge is the area where horse and carriage traffic was handled in a series of docks. Most of the horse-boxes visible are of Stroudley design, although the nearest is of Craven origin. Trolleys on the platform are laden with the trunks and portmanteaux without which no self-respecting Victorian would travel. The 'Gladstone' takes water while a vendor sells refreshments to the passengers from a wicker tray strapped around his neck.
NRM Burtt 1719

Plate 45. A Craven 2–4–0 stands at the down platform on the London side with a Victoria–Hastings train, probably in 1886. Photographs of locomotives at work of this vintage are rare, which makes this picture especially welcome. The engine has its driving wheel springs underhung and the cut-outs in the sides of its splashers remain, which suggests that it may have been No. 174, built at Brighton Works in 1864, the engine involved in the 1879 Lewes boiler explosion. No. 174 was finally withdrawn in 1889. A Stroudley 'D1', No. 297 *Bonchurch* is in the centre of the photograph, and a third engine, a 'Terrier', is at the head of the Seaford branch train under the overall roof on the bay platform. The negative at the National Railway Museum appears to be a copy and lacks the definition of the original Bedford print from which this illustration was prepared.

NRM Burtt 1718

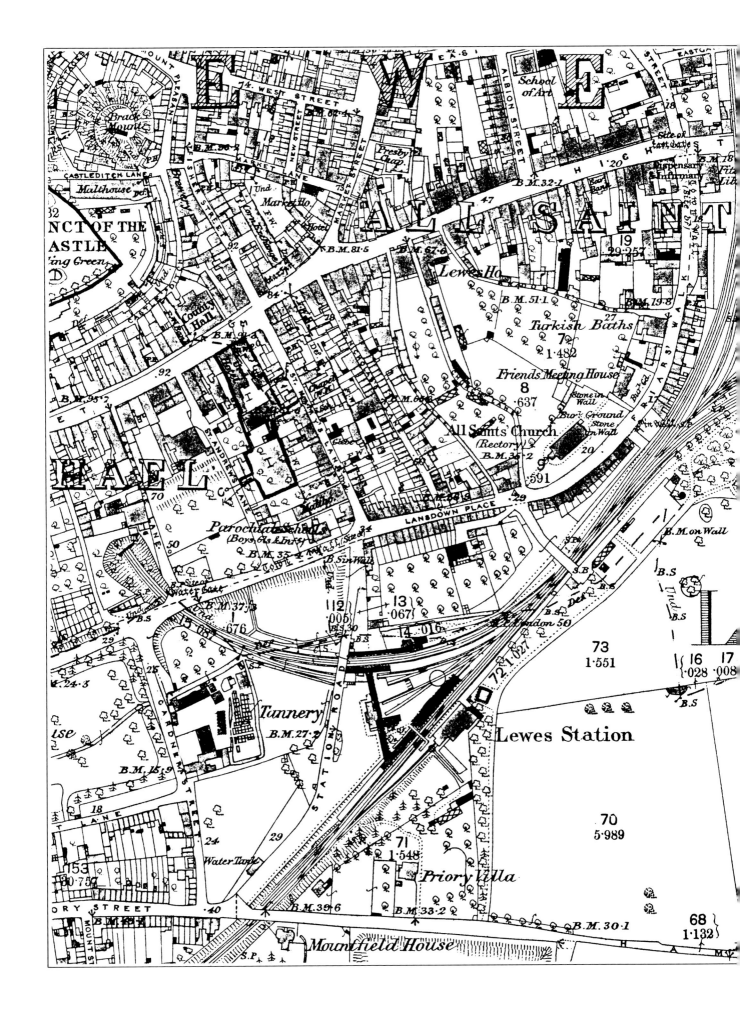

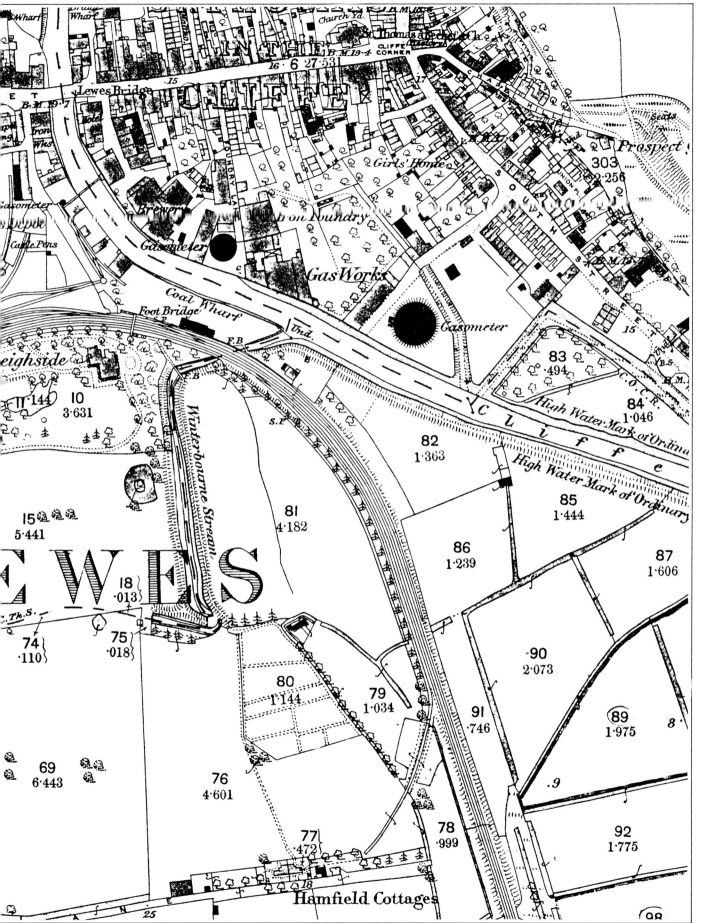

Taken from 25 inch Ordnance Survey for 1873. Crown Copyright reserved.

Plate 46. The Brighton line platforms at Lewes in June 1888. The two gentlemen are, on the left, Station Inspector Hayden. The train comprises Stroudley 1st/2nd composite, a third, and a luggage van of the earliest Stroudley pattern, with flat sides and beading extending the full height of the vehicle. Remarkably, the body of a similar van was discovered recently in Sussex and has now been restored. Beyond is Lansdown Place with the bridge carrying the drive to 'Leighside'. The house was built by Bernard Godlee, a retired lime merchant and Lewes councillor, who was one of the main advocates of the building of the line from Brighton to Hastings. Among his other business interests was a directorship in the Newhaven Harbour Company. He died on 9th December 1892. Through this can be seen the 1846 goods warehouse and the old route to Uckfield diverging on the left. The ironwork for the new bridge carrying the Uckfield route is in place and the end of the transhipment shed, put up in 1884, can just be made out. Next to this is the small signal box, half tucked under the bridge, which survived well into the 1930s as staff accommodation.

NRM Burtt 1716

Plate 47. The 1857 station, taken from the bridge at the north end carrying Southover Road over the railway, c.1888. A 'Gladstone' stands in the up London platform with a train that includes a Craven vehicle of the 1860s as the third carriage. What is now the cattle market was then a field. In the foreground is a small ground frame controlling the points and signals of the north end of the station. The bridge in the centre of the photograph is that carrying Station Road, and the station buildings can be seen behind it.

Plate 48. Lewes Junction signal box was of considerable importance in the development of railway signalling. Dating from the rebuilding of the station in 1857, it was one of the first boxes to be constructed by the signalling pioneer and LB & SCR employee, William Saxby.

Plate 49. Rebuilding is well in hand in this view of the east end of the station in 1888. The contractors have run their tracks off the erstwhile engine shed road and an embankment is being formed as the first stage in levelling for the new lines. The work is being carried out in the former grounds of Priory Villa. The contractor's locomotive is just visible in the centre background. *NRM Burtt 1715*

Plate 50. A 'G' class hauls the first train through the rebuilt Lewes station on 17th June 1889 — a difficult picture to take as, early in the morning, one faces directly into the sun at this point. The train is the up Continental from Newhaven, the first two vehicles being passengers' luggage vans, followed by two high-roofed vans whose purpose remains something of a mystery. They look as though they ought to be some form of covered carriage truck, although very short for this use. However, another photograph reveals that they did not possess end doors, which would rule out this function. No diagrams of them have come to light as yet and they constitute quite a puzzle. Next comes a Stroudley 6-wheel brake and a line of four-wheelers. The station still has an unfinished look to it with headless columns for oil lamps on the platform to the left. At this stage, there were no awnings to protect passengers from the weather. J. Anscombe's tender for the roof on the central platform had been accepted on 21st May 1889 but the company experienced great difficulty in securing the completion of the work. By 21st December, only the columns had been completed and then, on 11th February 1890, it was reported that Anscombe, who had carried out much work for the LB & SCR, had died, leaving his affairs in some disorder. The well-known builders, James Longley & Co. of Crawley, were called in to complete the station in 1891. The remaining contractors for the rebuilding work were Joseph Firbank for all trackwork, the new Uckfield incline and bridges, the aforementioned Longleys for all station buildings, Messrs. Matthew T. Shaw & Co. of Millwall, London, for the new Station Road bridge and associated ironwork, and John Every of the Phoenix Iron Works, Lewes, for stanchions and iron columns.
NRM Burtt 1720

Plate 51. The equivalent first down train (described by Bedford as a newspaper train) coming in from the north, hauled by a 'G' class 2–2–2. The platform on the far right is the old down London Platform which was to be turned into a cattle dock. The site now forms part of the station car park. A considerable crowd watches from the bridge as the train passes the new Lewes North signal box, which controlled the divergence of the old and new lines and was replaced by the Southern Railway in 1934. The NRM negative appears to be a copy as it lacks the definition of the Bedford print from which this illustration has been reproduced. *NRM Burtt 1721*

THE OLD CURVE

Plate 52. No. 329 *Stephenson* negotiates the old curve on 30th May 1889. Taken from a footbridge that formerly crossed the line here, this is one of Bedford's finest compositions, the train being perfectly framed by the foliage either side of the line. The second vehicle is a London & North Western Railway saloon. On the left is the high garden wall of 'Leighside' which the railway skirts. The sharpness of the curve is emphasised by the check rail, and, together with the equally tight radius through the old station, serves to explain why the LB & SCR was anxious to re-route the line. The new bridge carrying the Uckfield line runs across the view, and the goods 'yard is filled with LB & SCR 'Open A's and Stroudley vans, all in light grey with black ironwork. Just beyond the bridge is the roof of the goods warehouse and the houses in Friars Walk. *NRM Burtt 1762*

Plate 53. *Grosvenor* a little further along the old curve, with the slate-clad Bear Yard corn and seed stores of William and Edmund Strickland (still extant) in the background and the railway cottage on the left. Taken in 1889, probably on 7th June. *NRM Burtt 1763*

Plate 54. Another train in the same position on 7th June 1889, hauled by No. 188 *Allen Sarle*. The leading van is well down on its springs. *NRM Burtt 1764*

41

Plate 55. Looking east from the footbridge on 30th May 1889. No. 211 *Cavendish*, one of the 'Richmond' class which were the predecessors to the 'Gladstones', hauls an up train. The engine bears the family name of the Duke of Devonshire. There are very few known photographs of this class in motion, although there are a number of them standing idle outside locomotive sheds. Three 'Open A's stand in the approach to the yard, equipped with a chain to support a tarpaulin instead of a bar, as was later practice. The first vehicle in the train is another of the early Stroudley luggage vans.

NRM Burtt 1761

Plate 56. Still further along the curve on the same day, another 'Gladstone' on a train which has at its head one of the final pattern of Craven luggage vans. These vans, built in the late 1860s, were amongst the last Craven vehicles to survive, disappearing in 1892-4. The train is passing Lewes Good Yard signal box, a timber Saxby and Farmer structure opened in March 1878 and closed in 1966.

NRM Burtt 1760

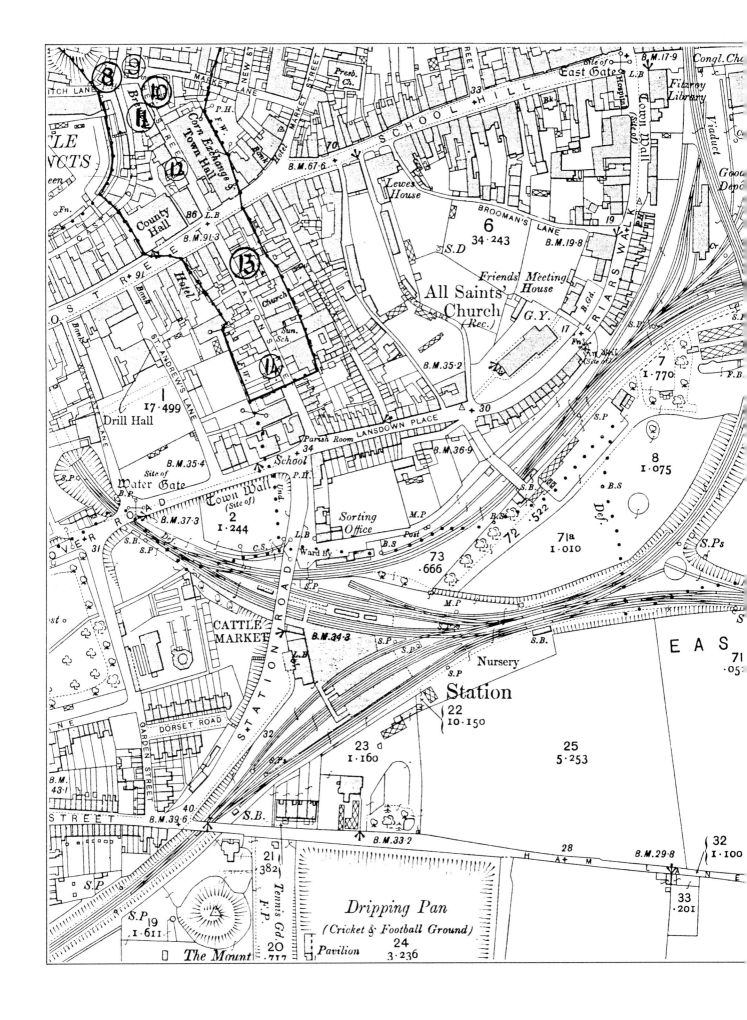

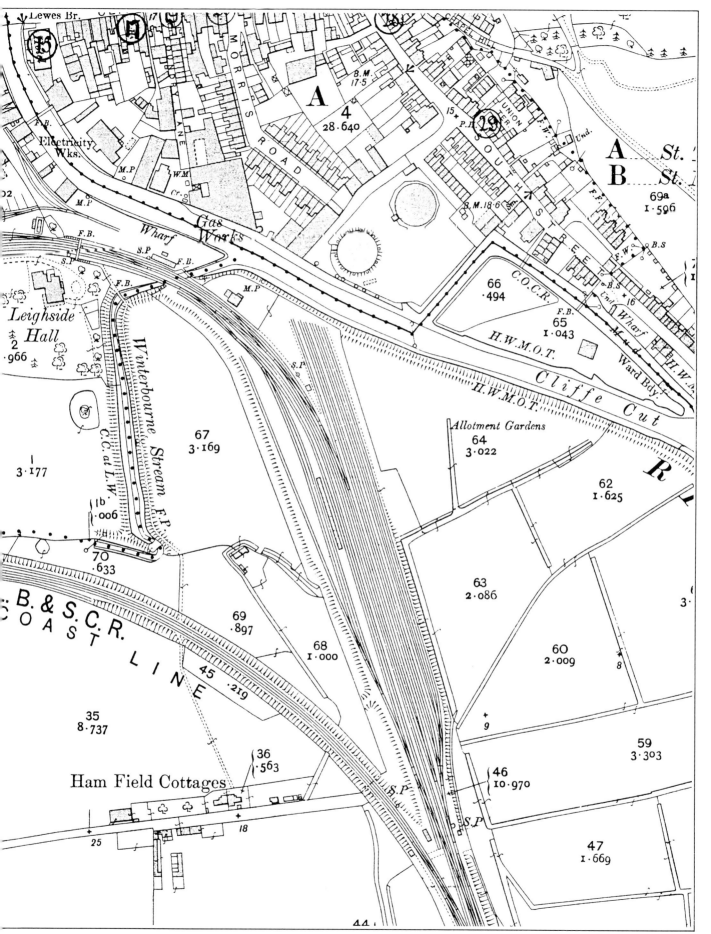

Lewes Br.

Electricity Wks.

MORRIS ROAD

B.M 17·5

A
4
28·640

BM.18·6

A ____ St.
B ____ St.

69a
1·596

Gas Works

Wharf

SOUTH STREET

66
·494

C.O.C.R.

65
1·043

H.W.M.O.T.

Cliffe Cut

Ward Bdy.

Leighside Hall
2
·966

Winterbourne Stream F.P.

C.C. at L.W.

1
3·177

1b
·006

67
3·169

Allotment Gardens
64
3·022

62
1·625

R.

70
·633

B. & S.C.R.
COAST LINE

69
·897

68
1·000

45
·219

63
2·086

60
2·009

9

59
3·303

35
8·737

36
·563

Ham Field Cottages

46
10·970

S.P.

25

18

47
1·669

44

Plate 57. The down Newhaven boat train crosses Southerham bridge on a misty morning c.1891 following the introduction of Pullman cars on a permanent basis on the service that year. The locomotive is again No. 326 *Grosvenor.*

NRM Burtt 1754

SOUTHERHAM

Plate 58. At the same location, a Stroudley single pulls a train of fourteen vehicles bound for Eastbourne and Hastings.

NRM Burtt 1753

Plate 59. An excellent view of the boat train c.1891 with the two 6-wheel lavatory composites Nos. 271/2 built to Diagram 42/84 in 1882, and, in the centre of the train, the Pullman *Victoria*.

Plate 60. The lines to Eastbourne and to Newhaven and Seaford diverge at Southerham Junction. Looking eastwards, the Eastbourne line is on the left and Newhaven on the right. A group of platelayers stand next to a local train headed by a 'D' tank. The signal box controlling the junction was constructed in 1874 and was fitted with a 22-lever frame. It was one of a relatively small number of boxes put up at this period with vertical recessed panels in the framing (Cooksbridge, Slinfold, Baynards, Cranleigh, Bramley and Wonersh and Southwater are the other known examples). Its appearance disguised behind brickwork added as an anti-blast precaution in the Second World War, the box lasted until 1976. The pathway on the left leads to the signalmen's cottages which dated from 1861 when Jabez Reynolds was authorised to replace some old cottages which were then removed to Cooksbridge. The 1861 cottages have in turn been demolished.

NRM Burtt 1722

Plate 61. Lewes has over the years experienced some spectacular floods, notably from the railway point of view in 1891 and 1960. A down express gingerly negotiates the waters of the swollen Winterbourne as it leaves Lewes on 24th October 1891.

NEWHAVEN

Plate 62. Bedford stands on the down platform of Newhaven Harbour station to record No. 325 *Abergavenny* leaving with the up Continental train. The Continental station just visible behind the locomotive was completed in 1885 and completely destroyed by fire on Sunday, 21st November 1887. It was rebuilt to the original ornate design at the original cost by Messrs. Longley of Crawley. Newhaven Harbour South signal box, whose roof can be seen above the first van, followed in 1886. Of all the buildings in the picture, it is the only one still extant. Due to the tidal nature of the service, passengers might find themselves spending quite a good deal of time in Newhaven which was not the most hospitable of places, and the company provided a palatial hotel, the London and Paris, for them. A portion of it can be seen on the right. It was built by John Fabian who had won a competition held in 1847 in which a premium of £100 was awarded for the best design. The building was finally demolished in the 1950s. The verandah alongside it was added in 1886 and the former wooden customs shed beyond was constructed in the early 1860s with a barrel vaulted roof. This form of construction was particularly associated with harbour installations in England and was also frequently found in industrial premises in Ireland. Most of the buildings at Newhaven were constructed of wood because of the lack of firm foundations. Outside the shed one can see a shunting horse and the Dieppe-bound steamer. Returning to the train, the first two vehicles are interesting, being two of the high roof vans seen in *Plate 50*. *NRM Burtt 3389*

Plate 63. Some confusion surrounds the history of the locomotive shed at Newhaven. On 21st June 1887, a disastrous fire occurred. According to local newspaper reports, only the paint shop and stores of the Marine Department were destroyed. However, the LB & SCR's Engineering Committee Minutes state the locomotive shops and stores were destroyed by fire. This contradiction is not fully resolved. What we can be sure of is that James Longley was awarded a contract in the sum of £594 to build a new engine shed when the Engineering Committee of the LB & SCR Board met on 26th October. A month later, they put in a successful tender for the new locomotive workshops. The new shed was of economical construction in corrugated iron, with the shops in brick, and still exists today largely unaltered. Bedford's picture of 1888 shows the shed brand new and as yet unsullied by smoke. *NRM Burtt 1759*

COOKSBRIDGE

Plate 64. Cooksbridge and Haywards Heath were Bedford's chosen locations for his experiments in high speed photography. A down train in the charge of an unidentified 'Gladstone' rushes through Cooksbridge station in 1891. The train lacks the Pullman car usually found in the set and the ensemble contrasts with the Billinton bogie vehicles employed just a few years later. A bowler-hatted gentleman, who may be an inspector, peers out of the cab. *NRM Burtt 1771*

Plate 65. A similar subject to the previous photograph but a Pullman car is included in the train. *NRM Burtt 1774*

Plate 66. No. 187 *Philip Rose* on the boat train. Sir Philip Rose was senior partner in the firm of Norton, Rose and Brewer, the LB & SCR's solicitors (still prominent as commercial solicitors today under the name of Norton Rose) and was well-known as a confidant of Disraeli.

NRM Burtt 1775

Plate 67. Bedford took this and the next three photographs from the up platform. The boat train was on this occasion hauled by a single. In the bay is a row of 'Open A' wagons. Chatfields, the timber merchants, moved their main depot from St. John's Wharf, Lewes, to Cooksbridge in December 1882 and continue to run their business from the same site today. The photograph was taken prior to 1889 as in that year, the rather crude corrugated iron waiting shed seen on the left was replaced by a new wooden structure built by G. Chapman.

NRM Burtt 1758

Plate 68. A similar view but with an 'Open D' wagon clearly displaying LB & SCR wagon livery — light grey with black ironwork.

NRM Burtt 1756

Plate 69. The large single *Grosvenor* with driver Schofield on the footplate hauling the Continental. Bedford stated that the train was travelling at 60 mph.

NRM Burtt 1765

Plate 70. A 'D' tank which, according to the slide's caption, is passing Cooksbridge at 60 mph.

Plate 71. The other end of Cooksbridge station with the up boat train racing through behind a single. The signal box on the left is of the same design as that at Southerham Junction and was built in 1872. In later years, it had vertical tongue and groove boarding rather than the style of panelling seen here and looked quite different in appearance as a result. The nameboard on the box is of the early pattern with white lettering on a blue background. The LB & SCR started to fit these enamelled iron boards to their signal boxes in 1875. Cooksbridge box was only demolished in 1986. Beyond it is a typical pair of 'Brighton' crossing gates and, in the distance, the rolling South Downs.

ROYAL TRAINS

Plate 72. *Grosvenor* takes the Prince of Wales back from a day at Lewes races to Eastbourne where he was staying with the Duke of Devonshire. The date is 20th June 1891 and the location the curve just south of Lewes station. The stock consists of two Diagram 47 brakes, two 6-wheel firsts, the 1877 Stroudley royal saloon and beyond it, a 1st class saloon. The train carries the special train headcode of three double diamond boards and bears the Prince of Wales's feathers at the base of the chimney to indicate that he is aboard.
NRM Burtt 1770

Plate 73. A second picture of the same train. The house in the background is 'Leighside' which was practically surrounded by railways once the new line was built.

Plate 75. *Below:* 'D3' *Haslemere* pulls past Lewes Junction signal box on 6th August 1897 with the royal train. The Prince of Wales was staying on board the steam yacht *Rena* owned by the Baron de Rothschild which had brought him to Newhaven. The train provided a shuttle service for him and his guests for the duration of the stay to enable them to visit the Lewes races. The Prince is probably not on board as his feathers are not displayed.

Plate 74. An earlier view, taken in 1889 of the LB & SCR royal train entering Lewes from the west behind an unidentified 'Gladstone'.

Plate 76. An animated scene on the up London platform at the rebuilt Lewes station as the Prince of Wales arrives for his visit to the races during 1897.

COAST AND DOWNLAND

Plate 77. South of Southerham Junction, No. 174 *Fratton* hauls the Newhaven boat train, the third vehicle being one of two 6-wheel lavatory composites, Nos. 271/2 built in 1882 to Diagram 42/84. These were the only carriages fitted with toilets at the time on the LB & SCR apart from special vehicles and saloons. Someone has forgotten to close one of the oil lamp covers.

NRM Burtt 1776

Plate 78. No. 218 *Beaconsfield* enters Glynde from the east c.1891. The siding on the right leads to Balcombe Chalk Pit and another hidden behind the train went to a clay pit. Examples of an LB & SCR telegraph post, 'whistle' board, gradient post and buffer stop can be seen together with a typical Saxby & Farmer home signal of the period.

Plate 79. Another view at the same location, with a Stroudley single heading a lengthy train which includes a seven-compartment First of 1880, one of a group of vehicles which were the first bogie carriages to be built for the LB & SCR.

Plate 80. Bedford seemed fascinated with the boat trains, taking many more views of them than the ordinary expresses. Here is a single taking the up boat express through Hamsey cutting, north of Lewes, c.1892.

NRM Burtt 1755

Plate 81. Moving further afield, we have a Royal Special for the Shah of Persia which ran from Brighton to Portsmouth on 29th July 1889. The precise location of this photograph is unknown. The Shah had arrived in Brighton on 26th July for the weekend. He was to board the Royal Yacht for Cowes and Osborne House and from there to sail to Cherbourg and thence by rail to Paris. The engine bears a special train headcode but no indication of any English royal presence. During his stay, the Shah was so horrified by the speed of the train that had taken him from Portsmouth to London that, on arriving at Victoria station, he requested the summary execution of the driver responsible! He was told politely that that was not the way we did things here.

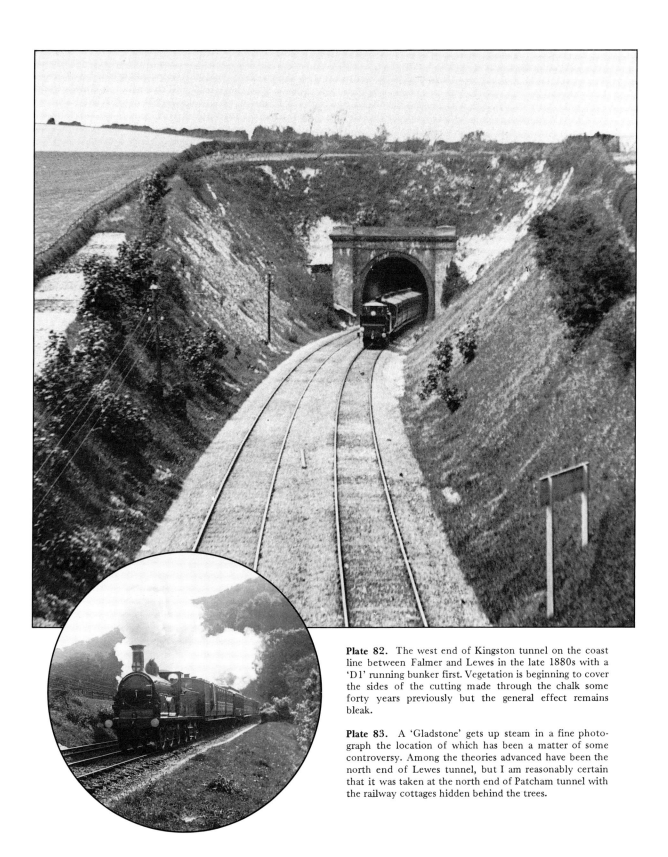

Plate 82. The west end of Kingston tunnel on the coast line between Falmer and Lewes in the late 1880s with a 'D1' running bunker first. Vegetation is beginning to cover the sides of the cutting made through the chalk some forty years previously but the general effect remains bleak.

Plate 83. A 'Gladstone' gets up steam in a fine photograph the location of which has been a matter of some controversy. Among the theories advanced have been the north end of Lewes tunnel, but I am reasonably certain that it was taken at the north end of Patcham tunnel with the railway cottages hidden behind the trees.

Plate 84. A perpetual hazard for the action photographer over the years was the likelihood of the wind blowing the wrong way at the wrong time, causing the engine's exhaust to obscure much of the train. Such was evidently the case in this study of a 'Gladstone' north of Patcham on an up Pullman Limited train.

NRM Burtt 1772

HAYWARDS HEATH

Plate 85. The heavy 8.45 a.m. businessmen's express, unofficially called the 'City Limited', from Brighton stirs up the dust as it rushes through Haywards Heath in one of the finest of Bedford's action photographs. The train divided at East Croydon with Pullman cars *Victoria* and *Alexandria* together with the main part of the train working through to London Bridge. The date is between 1888 and 1893 as in 1888 an overall roof spanning the tracks was removed and replaced by the awnings seen here and in the latter year the up platform was widened. *NRM Burtt 1768*

Plate 86. *Grosvenor* turns up in so many of the photographs that one feels that Bedford had a particular liking for the engine. Here it is crossing the Balcombe Road bridge a little to the north of Haywards Heath station in 1889. According to Bedford's note on a lantern slide, the speed was 61 mph. So precise! The train was the Brighton Pullman, comprising the set introduced the previous December: parlour cars *Princess* and *Albert Victor*, and the kitchen car *Prince*, together with the generator/luggage van popularly known as a 'Pullman Pup', and a fourth Pullman.

NRM Burtt 1767

Plate 87. The same train but hauled by an unidentified 'Gladstone'. First class compartment carriages were added to all Pullman trains from 1st December 1882 following complaints about the lack of privacy in the open saloons of the Pullman cars. *NRM Burtt 1769*

Plate 88. Virtually identical to the previous photograph – only the exhaust differs. *NRM Burtt 1779*

Plate 89. A later photograph giving a closer view of the train. The 'Open A' bearing a tarpaulin is in the livery style introduced c.1895 with 'LB & SC Ry' superseding the earlier style seen on the wagon next to it, 'Open D' 5007.
NRM Burtt 1778

Plate 90. Another view of a train coming into Haywards Heath from the north. It is composed of the Brighton Pullman set supplemented by ordinary stock at the rear. The 'Pullman Pup' has been rebuilt with full width vestibules and the date is post 1894 as the last vehicle is a double-ended luggage brake van, the first of which appeared in that year. The newly constructed houses of Millgreen Road and College Road can be seen at the base of the embankment.

EXPRESSES AND EXCURSIONS

Plate 91. A well-known study and one of the few Bedford photographs to have been reproduced in several books; the last train over the old timber bridge carrying the west coast line over the River Adur at Shoreham at 4.30 p.m. on 8th June 1892. No. 186 *De La Warr* heads a train entirely composed of Stroudley stock with one of the early flat-sided luggage vans and a horse-box bringing up the rear. *NRM Burtt 1773*

Plate 92. A later view, east of Southerham (the box is visible on the left) has an unidentified 'Gladstone' at the head of a rake of Billinton stock. After the luggage van follow two 49ft First/Second composites of Diagram 65/88. *NRM Burtt 1777*

Plate 93. An up excursion train drawn by a Stroudley single near Southerham Junction. The sanding jets are working furiously. The luggage van is of Stroudley design, followed by a Billinton close-coupled suburban block train set, one of twenty-seven coach sets built by the Birmingham Railway Carriage & Wagon Co. between 1900 and 1901 for London suburban services. The headcode shows that the train is a relief working and will travel via the Quarry line bypassing the busy junction at Redhill.

NRM Burtt 2146

Plate 94. A single working hard with a heavy London-bound express made up of Billinton stock as it heads out of Eastbourne under Whitley Road Bridge in the 1890s.

THE 1897 ROYAL TRAIN

Construction of a new five-carriage royal train set commenced in 1897 and was completed in December 1898. Its first trial, a round trip from Brighton to Portsmouth, thence to Victoria and back to Brighton, took place on 15th January 1899. The train was first used by the Prince of Wales and his guests when they were carried from Victoria to the spring race meeting at Epsom Downs on 19th April 1899.

Plates 95 & 96. Bedford was a little late in exposing the first of this pair of photographs, in which 'B2' No. 202 *Trevethick* leaving Eastbourne. Nevertheless it provides a good view of the new train and emphasises the extra width of the royal saloon which was 9in wider than the other four carriages in the set. The train in this photograph and the next is conveying guests to Compton Place, the Eastbourne home of the Duke of Devonshire. The second photograph shows the splendid royal train drawn by 'B4' No. 42 *His Majesty* pulling out of Eastbourne with the Eastbourne Water Works Co.'s pumping station in the background. The headcode indicates that there is no royal presence on the train.

THE MARSH PERIOD

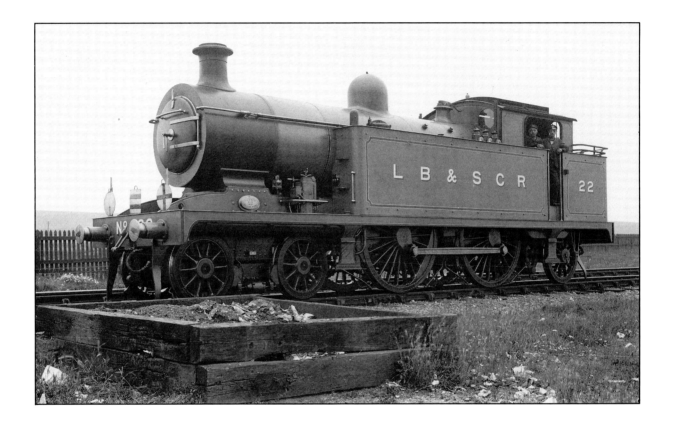

Plates 97-99. Bedford was evidently fascinated with the new tank engines designed by Douglas Earle Marsh. Their arrival prompted him to start taking railway photographs again after a break of some years. Here we have three portraits of No. 22, the second of the excellent 'I3' class and the first to be superheated, in works grey livery at Newhaven on 13th August 1908. The engine retained this livery for five months. The customs shed, opened in 1888 when the new wharves across Mill Reach were constructed, is in the background of the second view. *NRM Burtt 2154, 55, 56*

Plate 98.

LB&SCR

No. 2

Plate 99.

Plate 100. No. 80 of the same class soon after entering service in 1910. Differences from No. 22 include the positioning further forward of the leading steps, the rounding of the lower corners of the buffer beams with the front guard irons set behind the buffer beam and the absence of the handrail on the front of the tanks.

Plate 101. One of the least successful of the Marsh tanks was the under-boilered '14' class of which No. 33 is seen outside the customs shed at Newhaven on a winter's day soon after it was turned out by Brighton works in November 1908. The engine is in original form with brakes on the front bogie wheels, a fitment soon removed. *NRM Burtt 1241*

Plate 102. Southerham bridge being crossed on 11th August 1908 by 'Gladstone' No. 190 *Arthur Otway*, painted in the umber livery but otherwise largely as built. Arthur Otway was the Deputy Chairman of the LB & SCR at this period. *NRM Burtt 2147*

Plate 103. Named after its designer, No. 66 *Billinton* (formerly *Balmoral*) on an Eastbourne–Victoria express between Eastbourne and Hampden Park. The engine was one of the few to receive a name after the general practice of naming engines ceased in 1905. The coaches forming set train 51 have the high semi-elliptical roof introduced by A. H. Panter in 1905 which took full advantage of the loading gauge. The leading vehicle is a lavatory brake third of Diagram 121/190, one of 18 built in 1906. *NRM Burtt 2148*

Plate 104. At the same spot, 'I2' No. 14 on the Sunny South Special, a working on which the engine was regularly employed at the time. The Sunny South Special was introduced experimentally in 1904 and, after its initial success, was run annually during the summer months until 1915. It was a through train consisting of London & North Western Railway stock from the North and the Midlands to the South Coast resorts, notably Brighton and Eastbourne. The train shown consists mainly of arc-roofed 50ft carriages built between 1897 and 1903. The first four are brake first/third composites to Diagram 216. Sixty of these were built in 1900-01 and were used extensively on through workings of this type.

NRM Burtt 2149

Plate 105. The celebrated 'B4' class No. 70 *Holyrood*, holder of the London to Brighton speed record of 48 minutes 41 seconds, giving an average speed of 62.5 mph. The record run was staged on 26th July 1903 to try and placate the growing demand for electrification and reduce support for a planned rival electric line to Brighton.

NRM Burtt 2150

Plate 106. Another study of the first superheated 'I3' No. 22 in the lined grey livery. It is passing cornfields as it draws into Cooksbridge, possibly on a test train as the stock is the brand new Newhaven Continental set No. 87. This set was built to carry the expected upsurge in traffic brought about by the decision to hold the 1908 Olympic Games in London at the White City Stadium. The two holes provided in the buffer beam to allow the removal of the pistons and rods from the cylinders, a feature unique to this engine, are clearly visible. *NRM Burtt 2151*

Plate 107. A rare Bedford failure. The focal plane shutter has distorted the engine.   *NRM Burtt 2152*

Plate 108. One of the happiest of Bedford's later compositions, the 1908 Newhaven boat train south of Southerham Junction, again headed by No. 22.
NRM Burtt 2153

Plate 109. 'I3' No. 87 on a Brighton—Victoria express between Balcombe Tunnel and Three Bridges c.1913.

Plate 110. 'B4' No. 73 with the Sunny South Special on the four-track section north of Balcombe tunnel c.1912. The LNWR carriages, with the exception of the twelve-wheeled restaurant car, are of the elliptical roof pattern introduced in 1907.

Plate 111. Having presumably secured his photograph of the Sunny South Special, a photographer is himself immortalised together with his large reflex camera. His identity is a mystery (he cannot be Bedford who took this photograph) but he serves to make a charming and unusual picture. A better view is obtained of the 8ft 6in wide elliptical roof carriages. They were narrower than the majority of LNWR coaches and were intended for through workings. The train is composed of three portions, the first including the restaurant car. Apart from that vehicle, all the carriages are 57ft brake first/second composites built to Diagram £13 in 1909 and comprise six out of the ten vehicles built to that diagram. The formation serves as a graphic reminder of how much luggage people used to take on their holidays.

Plate 112. Lewes tunnel south end on 10th October 1934, just before rebuilding work started in connection with the lengthening of the up platform.

Plate 113. The last steam-hauled 1.28 p.m. Victoria–Eastbourne train drawn by 'L' No. 332 passes Lewes on 6th July 1935. Although steam-hauled excursions, through services and boat trains continued to be seen at Lewes, Bedford managed to capture the first and last regular main line steam workings to use the 1889 station.

NRM Burtt 2166

Plate 114. Bedford was by no means alone in photographing the last steam workings; amongst those who joined him was Ronald Tomkins, a well-known member of the Stephenson Locomotive Society before the war, who has his back to us.

NRM Burtt 2167

Plate 115. Ex-London & South Western Railway 'L12' No. 433 at Southerham. The engine, built in 1905 and equipped with a superheater in 1919, has been modified to meet the Eastern Section loading gauge, being fitted with a short chimney and given a six-wheel tender. *NRM Burtt 2168*

Plate 116. 'Schools' class No. 919 *Harrow* with the 5.15 p.m. Victoria–Eastbourne at Souther-ham on 6th July 1935. *NRM Burtt 2169*

Plate 117. 'Baltic' No. 2331 passes Southerham on the last steam-hauled working of the 5.06 p.m. London Bridge—Eastbourne of 5th July 1935. The photograph was taken at 1/100th at f8.

NRM Burtt 2170

Plates 118, 119 & 121. Three views of a veteran 'D' tank No. 2232 (formerly *Lewes*) that Bedford had photographed just a hundred yards away when it was still only a few years old. No. 232 was the first 'D' tank to be fitted with motor train equipment in November 1905 and received the Marsh boiler seen here in 1922. *NRM Burtt 2176, 2174*

Plate 120. The first of the new electric trains, composed of a 6-PUL unit, pauses at the down London platform.

NRM Burtt 2177

Plate 121.

Plate 123. Another race special of 10th August 1935, this time hauled by 'K' class No. 2345. Again the location is the water meadows of the Ouse just north of Lewes.

Plate 122. Steam did not completely disappear from the area with the Eastbourne electrification. 'King Arthur' class No. 766 *Sir Geraint*, with the 4000-gallon six-wheel tender with which it was fitted from 1929 to 1937, heads a Pullman race special north of Lewes tunnel on 10th August 1935.

NRM Burtt 2172

Plate 124. A 6-PUL set draws out of the north end of Lewes tunnel, a few minutes walk away from Bedford's house.

NRM Burtt 2179

Plate 125. A 6-PAN unit at Southerham bridge, the silver paint on the roof gleaming in the sun. 8th July 1935.

NRM Burtt 2180

Plate 126. The first electric 5.20 p.m. Victoria–Eastbourne with a 5-PUL set leading. 8th July 1935.
NRM Burtt 2181

GREAT WESTERN RAILWAY

Plate 127. Like T. F. Budden, Bedford decided to record the last days of the Great Western broad gauge. He took just three photographs, probably in 1889. This is Castle Hill for Ealing Dean (later West Ealing), a station that did not change greatly for many years, the goods warehouse in the background only being demolished a few years ago. The locomotive is one of the noted 8ft 'Rovers' on a down express to the west, composed of convertible stock, headed by a 40ft van to Diagram K2, one of the five 7ft 6in high vehicles built in 1887 with elliptical roofs. As it has a double projection for the guard's look-out, it must be No. 174, the only van of this type so fitted. *NRM Burtt 1750*

Plate 128. Looking the other way, an up express rushes through the station, watched by railway staff. The extra width of the earlier pattern of convertible vehicles (which could be reduced in width by the removal of a section of the body) contrasts with the later design where the narrower bodies were mounted on broad gauge underframes. The 40ft van is from the same batch as the van in the previous photograph but is one of the five built with the earlier arc roof and, as it, too, has the double projection, it is likely to be No. 173. *NRM Burtt 1751*

Plate 129. For his third photograph, Bedford went to Ealing where he photographed an express entering from the east. *NRM Burtt 1749*

Plate 130. For the remainder of his GWR photographs, Bedford recorded the Royal Train. Here it is seen on unfamiliar territory, on the LB & SCR main line near Lewes. The engine bearing the LB & SCR headcode discs is No. 55 *Queen*, the locomotive usually employed on these duties, which was built in 1873 and seen here as reboilered in 1886. It was subsequently reboilered again in 1896 and withdrawn in 1905. The rolling stock making up the Royal Train is a real mixture; the leading vehicle is a flat-sided van of the 'sixties, then follows a six-wheel four-compartment first, a clerestory saloon, the 1874 royal saloon, a six-wheeled arc-roofed saloon, another clerestory saloon and a Diagram V2 luggage van. *NRM Burtt 1748*

Plate 131. The magnificent new Royal Train of 1897 races through West Ealing behind the elegant Dean single No. 3041 *The Queen*. The occasion is Queen Victoria's Diamond Jubilee and she is travelling from Windsor to Paddington on 21st June 1897, accompanied by the waves and greetings of her subjects. *NRM Burtt 1752*

Plate 132. A second view of the 1897 Royal Train, also near Ealing.

GREAT NORTHERN RAILWAY

Plate 133. Great Northern Railway Stirling 8-footer No. 666 outside King's Cross on 11th September 1891. The driver, William Edis, poses with an oil-can while his colleague stands on the footplate. No. 666 was one of a group of ten built between 1881 and 1883 and was one of the first of this class to be built without the distinctive slots in the driving wheel splashers that characterised the earlier members.
NRM Burtt 3419

Plate 134. An identical view without the driver. *NRM Burtt 3420*

Plate 135. In the same position is No. 230, a 7ft 6in single built in April 1887 and withdrawn in January 1907. *NRM Burtt 3421*

Plate 136. Eight-footer No. 2, built in December 1871 and as reboilered in 1888, heads the Manchester express through Hatfield in 1890, the first of three photographs depicting this train. The rolling stock is an intriguing mixture of the earlier arc-roofed stock and the semi-elliptical style that superseded it. In the centre of the train is the GNR/MS & LR joint first class dining carriage No. 950 built specially for this service at Gorton in 1884/5.

NRM Burtt 1740

Plate 137. The same train at the same spot but hauled by No. 231. Bedford clearly had a liking for these large singles. Two workmen are intently examining the base of a telegraph post on the right. *NRM Burtt 1741*

Plate 138. The same locomotive in full flight through New Barnet, again on the up Sheffield and Manchester express. Among the wagons in the yard are a standard GNR 8-ton van, a Newstead Colliery open wagon No. 161 and GNR coal wagon on the further siding and, on the nearer row, some GNR double bolster wagons (numbers visible being 16011 and 3679), a single bolster with dumb buffers and a mineral wagon of the characteristic Scottish short wheelbase type. *NRM Burtt 1742*

Plate 139. Another of the handsome eight-footers, No. 53, which entered service in 1875 and was the first of the class to be allocated to King's Cross shed, at New Barnet with a matching rake of six-wheeled stock on the 'Flying Scotsman'. Just over two years before the picture was taken, it had received a new boiler and replacement frames and was finally scrapped in 1906.
NRM Burtt 1743

MIDLAND RAILWAY

Plate 140. No. 1757 *Beatrice*, one of the only two Midland Railway locomotives to carry a name, was a popular subject for photographers. Named after Princess Beatrice, it was one of the 1885/6 batch of Johnson's supremely elegant 7ft 4—4—0s. *NRM Burtt 1746*

Plate 141. A splendid portrait of Johnson 4—2—2 No. 1871 of 1890 outside St. Pancras in 1892 that has been reproduced several times since the National Railway Museum 'discovered' Bedford's negatives. Essery and Jenkinson in their *Illustrated Review of Midland Locomotives* draw attention to the livery of the tender which is unique in that it has square corners to the panels of the lining. The signal box is equally singular on a railway that was so standardised in such respects. *NRM Burtt 3422*

Plate 142. This is an example of Bedford's practice of repeating photographs with just a change in the personnel on the footplate. *NRM Burtt 3423*

Plate 143. More humble, yet still a thing of great beauty, is the subject of this study, Johnson 0—4—4T No. 1550, used on suburban services through the widened lines as is evident from the condensing pipes. The effect of the polished brass on the splashers, the condensing pipes and on the cut-out numerals on the tanks, when combined with the richness of the crimson lake, must have made these engines an extraordinary sight as they plunged through the sulphurous tunnels on the way to Moorgate. The engine was built in 1882 and withdrawn in 1927. *NRM Burtt 1747*

Plate 144. Mill Hill c.1890 with a rebuilt Kirtley 2—4—0 of the '890' class piloting a Johnson 7ft '2183' class 4—4—0. The train is unfortunately half-hidden by the steam but the leading vehicle is probably one of the eighty 43ft brake thirds ordered in 1882, and the second, a clerestory-roofed 12-wheeler of the 1870s. *NRM Burtt 1745*

Plate 145. An unidentified Johnson single passing the same spot on an express of mixed 6-wheeled and bogie stock comprising a 25ft 4-wheeled passenger brake van, a 31ft composite, a 31ft lavatory third and, further down the train, a Pullman. *NRM Burtt 1744*